play BASS with...

5575

5575

play BASS with...
QUEENS OF THE STONE AGE
THE VINES
BOWLING FOR SOUP
JIMMY EAT WORLD
BLINK 182
THE HIVES
SUM 41

Wise Publications London / New York / Paris / Sydney / Copenhagen / Berlin / Madrid / Tokyo

Exclusive Distributors:
Music Sales Limited
8/9 Frith Street, London W1D 3JB, England.
Music Sales Pty Limited
120 Rothschild Avenue, Rosebery, NSW 2018, Australia.

Order No. AM976371
ISBN 0-7119-9814-0
This book © Copyright 2003 by Wise Publications.

Compiled by Nick Crispin.
Music arranged by Paul Townsend.
Music processed by Andrew Shiels.
Cover photograph courtesy of London Features International.

Printed in the United Kingdom by
Caligraving Limited, Thetford, Norfolk.

CD recorded, mixed and mastered by Jonas Persson.
Guitars by Arthur Dick.
Bass Guitar by Paul Townsend.
Drums by Brett Morgan.

Your Guarantee of Quality
As publishers, we strive to produce every book to the highest commercial standards.
The music has been freshly engraved and the book has been carefully designed to
minimise awkward page turns and to make playing from it a real pleasure.
Particular care has been given to specifying acid-free, neutral-sized paper made from
pulps which have not been elemental chlorine bleached.
This pulp is from farmed sustainable forests and was produced with special regard for the environment.
Throughout, the printing and binding have been planned to ensure a sturdy,
attractive publication which should give years of enjoyment.
If your copy fails to meet our high standards, please inform us and we will gladly replace it.

www.musicsales.com

play BASS with...

A.K.A. I-D-I-O-T

Words & Music by Randy Fitzsimmons

Intro

2 bar count in:

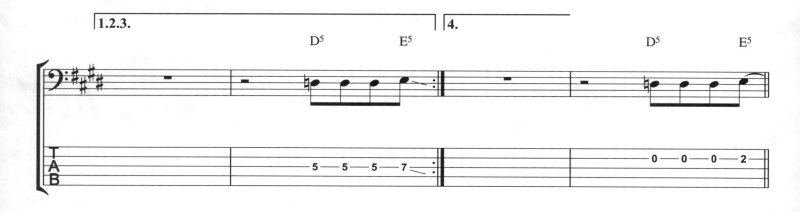

Verse

14

15

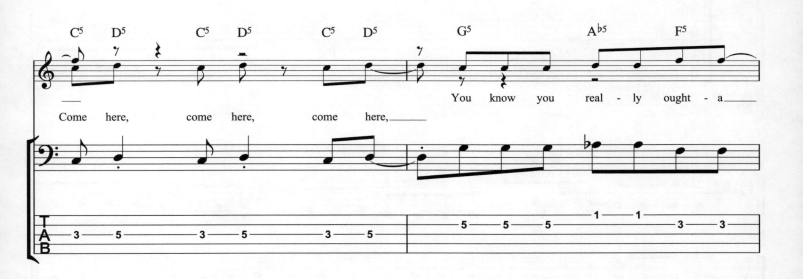

GIRL ALL THE BAD GUYS WANT

Words & Music by Jaret Reddick & Butch Walker

Intro

2 bar count in:

*4 string tab in italics

Verse

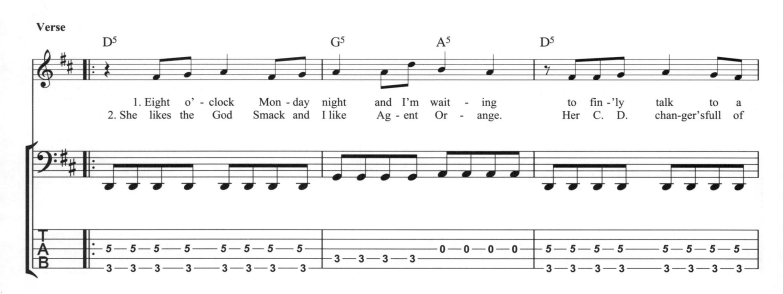

1. Eight o' - clock Mon - day night and I'm wait - ing to fin -'ly talk to a
2. She likes the God Smack and I like Ag - ent Or - ange. Her C. D. chan - ger's full of

Pre-chorus

girl a lit - tle cool - er than me. Her name is Mo - na, she's a rock - er with a nose ring,
sing - ers that are mad at their dad. She says she'd like to score some reef - er and a for - ty,

she wears a two way but I'm not quite sure what that means.
she'll nev - er know that I'm the best that she'll nev - er have.

And when she walks

all the wind blows and the an - gels sing, but

she does - n't no - tice me. 'Cause she's watch - ing wrest - ling, scream - ing ov - er

21

(G⁵)   (D⁵)   (E⁵)

in my eyes.   I can't grow a mous - tache and I ain't got no sea - son pass, all I got's a

(D/F♯)   (G⁵)   **Chorus**   E⁵

mo - ped, mo - ped, mo - ped. It's like a bad___ mov - ie, she's look - ing

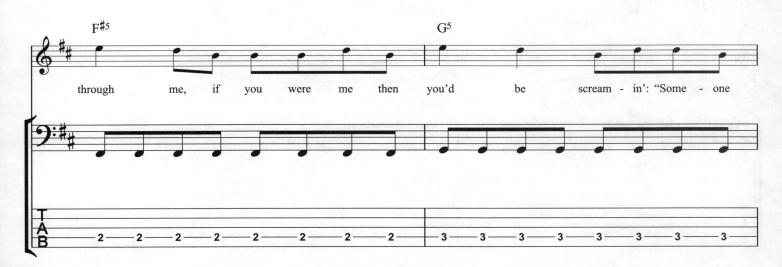

F♯⁵   G⁵

through me, if you were me then you'd be scream - in': "Some - one

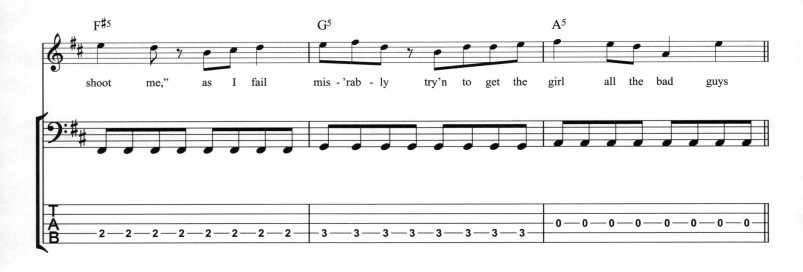

shoot me," as I fail mis-'rab-ly try'n to get the girl all the bad guys

Outro

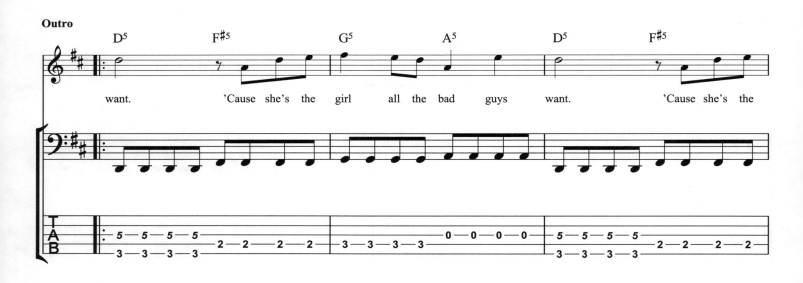

want. 'Cause she's the girl all the bad guys want. 'Cause she's the

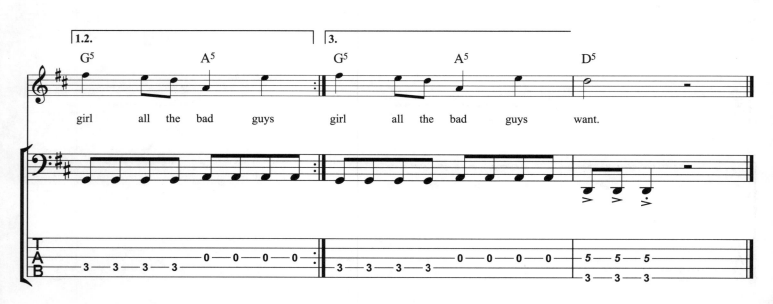

girl all the bad guys girl all the bad guys want.

IN TOO DEEP

Words & Music by Greig Nori & Deryck Whibley

Verse

2. Seem like each time____ I'm with you   I lose my mind____ be-cause I'm bend-ing ov-er back-wards to re-

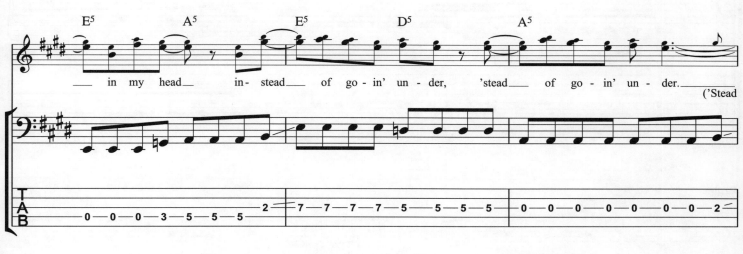

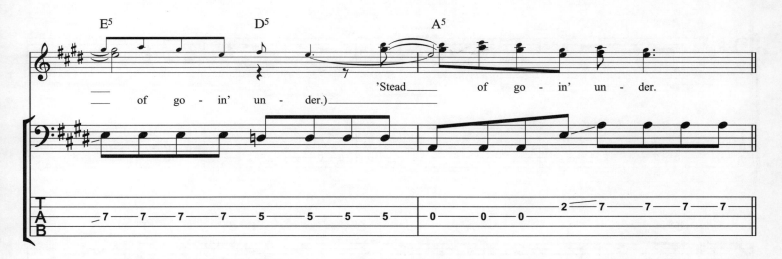

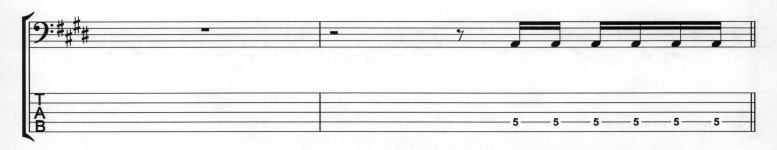

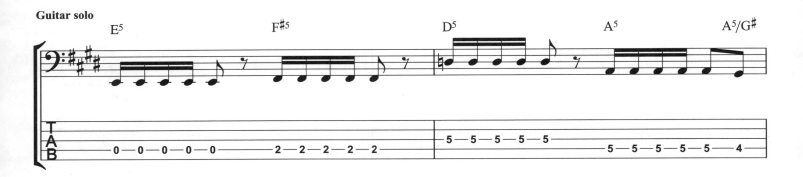

Guitar solo

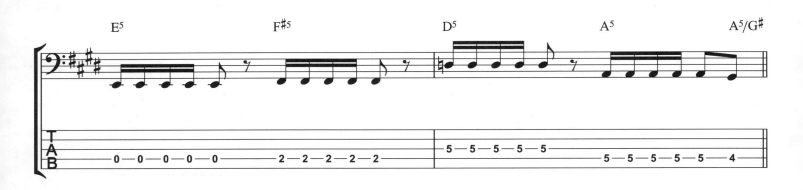

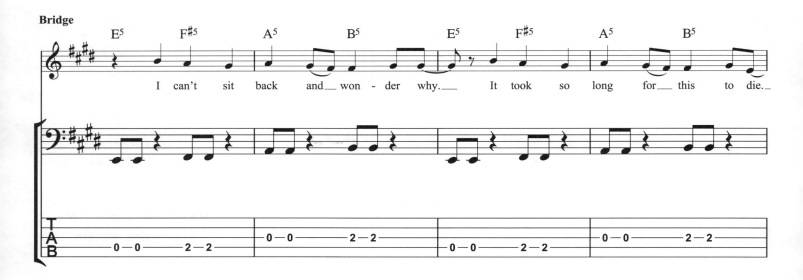

Bridge

I can't sit back and won - der why.__ It took so long for__ this to die.__

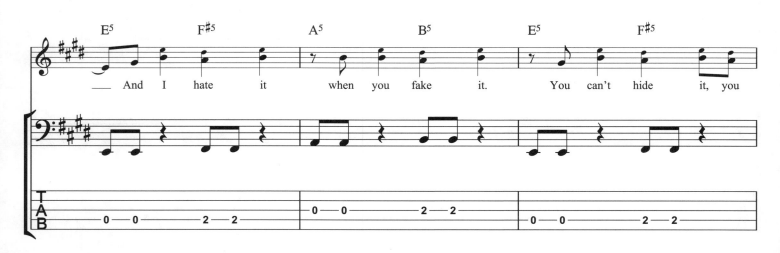

__ And I hate it when you fake it. You can't hide it, you

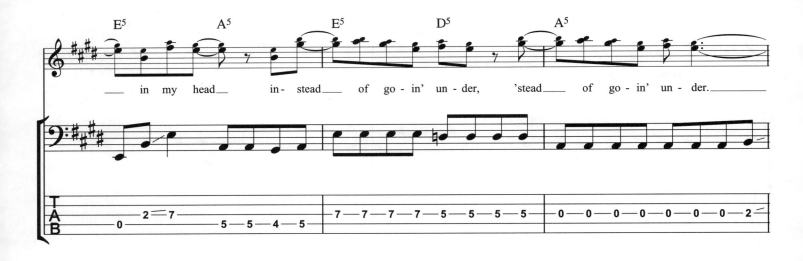

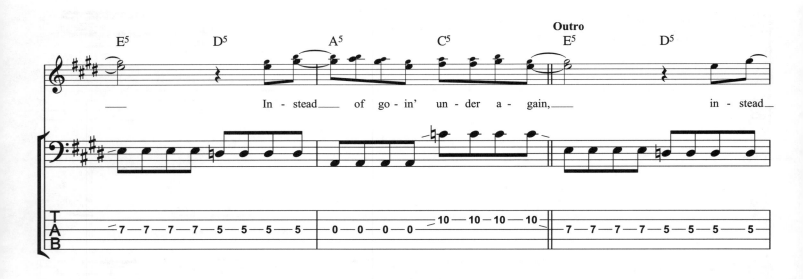

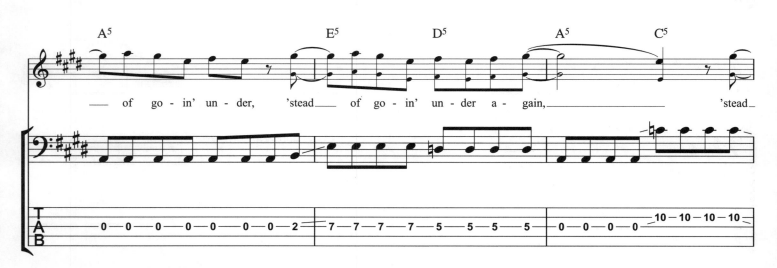

of go - in' un - der a - gain.

('Stead___ of go - in' un - der a - gain.)___

Tacet to end

THE MIDDLE

Words & Music by James Adkins, Thomas Linton, Richard Burch & Zachary Lind

Intro

2 bar count in:

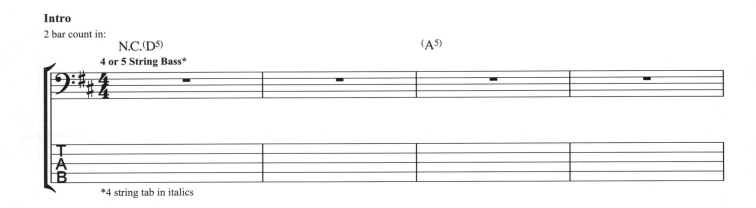

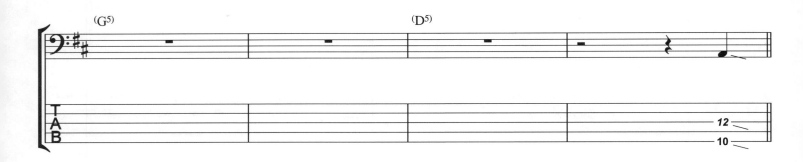

Verse

1.& Hey, _____ don't write your - self off yet,
2. Hey, _____ you know they're all the same,

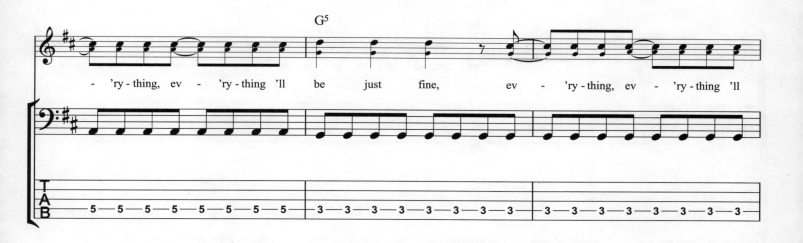

-'ry-thing, ev - 'ry-thing 'll   be   just   fine,   ev - 'ry-thing, ev - 'ry-thing 'll

Guitar solo

be   al - right,___ al - right.___

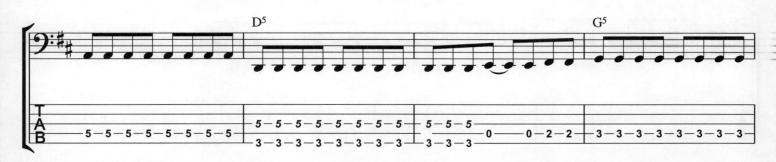

D.S. al Coda

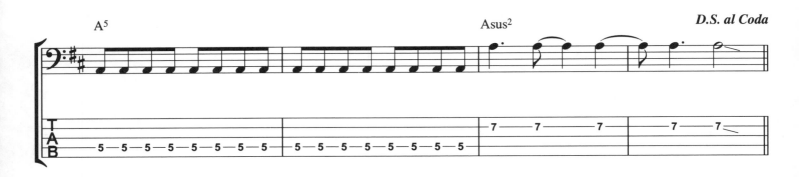

✦ **Coda**

Outro chorus

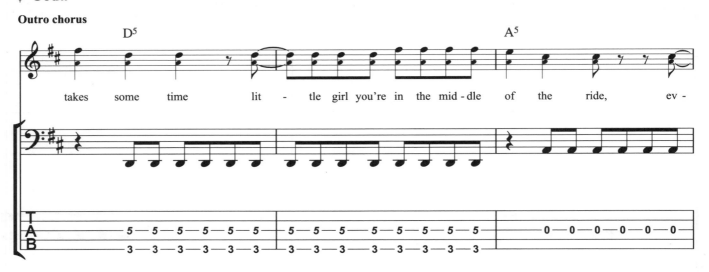

takes   some   time   lit - tle   girl you're in the mid - dle   of   the   ride,   ev -

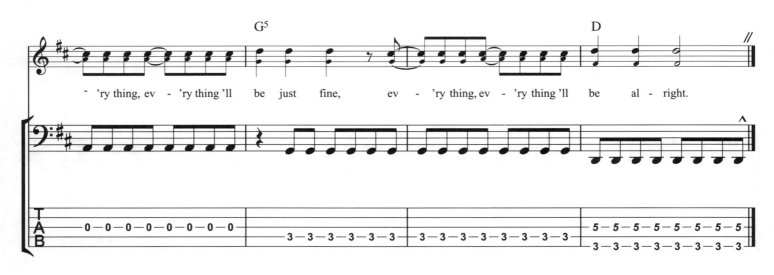

- 'ry thing, ev - 'ry thing 'll   be   just   fine,   ev - 'ry thing, ev - 'ry thing 'll   be   al - right.

THE ROCK SHOW

Words & Music by Mark Hoppus, Thomas Delonge & Travis Barker

Intro
2 bar count in:

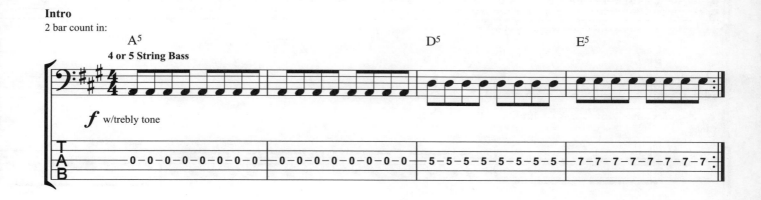

Verse

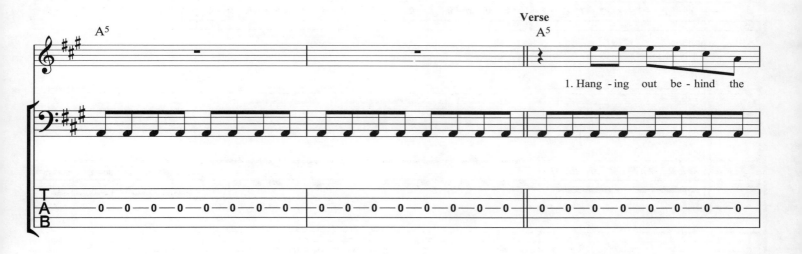

1. Hang - ing out be - hind the

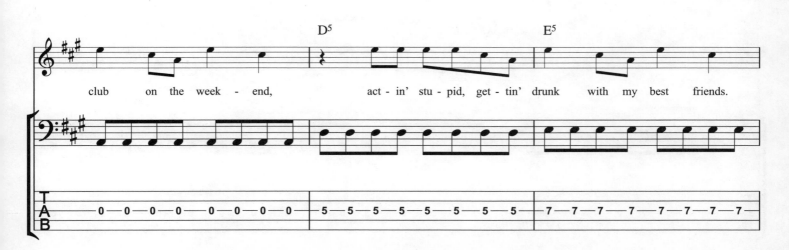

club on the week - end, act - in' stu - pid, get - tin' drunk with my best friends.

I could -n't wait   for the   sum - mer   and the   Warped   Tour.   I   re - mem - ber   it's the

first time   that   I   saw   her   there.

Verse

2. She's get - tin' kicked   out   of   school   'cause she's   fail   - ing.
3.   When   we   said   we   were   gon - na   move   to   Veg   -   as

41

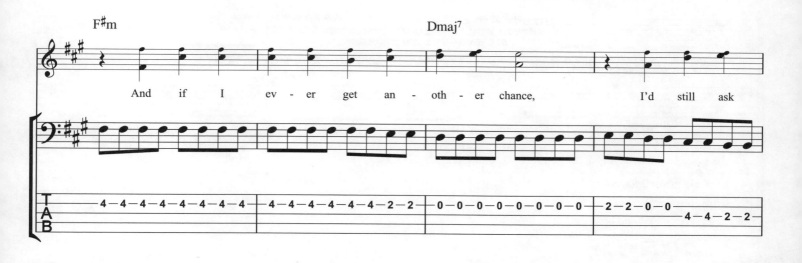

And if I ev - er get an - oth - er chance, I'd still ask

her to dance be - cause she kept me wait - ing. I

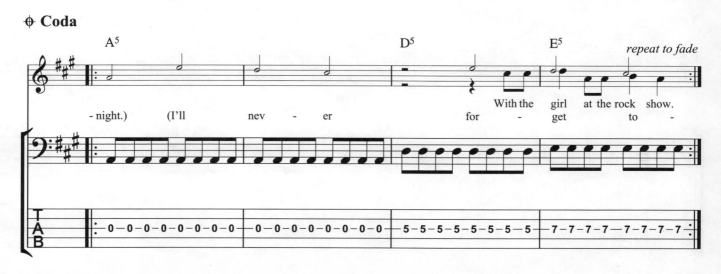

- night.) (I'll nev - er for - get to -

With the girl at the rock show.

NO ONE KNOWS

Words & Music by Josh Homme, Nick Oliveri & Mark Lanegan

Tune down 2 tones

④ = C   ② = B♭

③ = F   ① = E♭

Intro

2 bar count in:

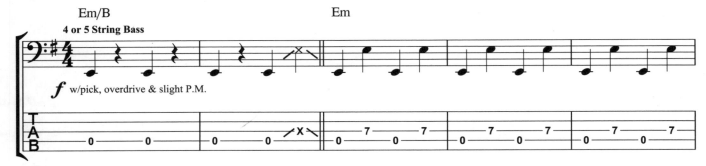

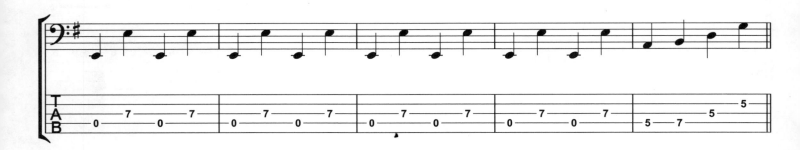

Verse

1. We got___ some rules___ to fol - low,
2. We get___ these pills___ to swal - low,

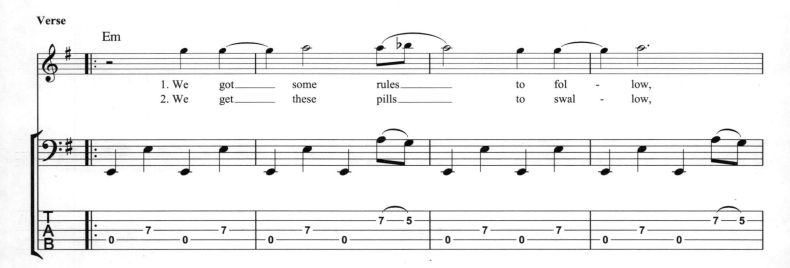

Plea - sant - ly cav -

-ing in.   I come_____ un - done._____

And I

re - a - lise you're____ mine.____

In -

BASS GUITAR
TABLATURE EXPLAINED

Bass Tablature is a four-line staff that graphically represents the bass fingerboard. By placing a number on the appropriate line, the string and fret of any note can be indicated. The number 0 represents an open string. For example:

3rd string, 3rd fret   4th string, open

SLIDE (not restruck): Strike the first note and then slide the same fret-hand finger up or down to the second note.

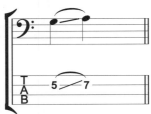

SLIDE (with restrike): Same as previous slide, except the second note is struck.

SLIDE: Slide up to the note indicated from a few notes below.

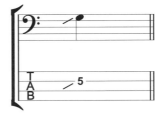

SLIDE: Strike the note indicated and slide up an indefinite number of frets.

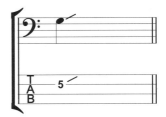

HAMMER-ON: Strike the first (lower) note with one finger, then sound the higher note (on the same string) with another finger by fretting it without picking.

PULL-OFF: Place both fingers on the notes to be sounded. Strike the first note and without picking, pull the finger off to sound the second lower note.

PALM-MUTE: The note is partially muted by the pick hand lightly touching the string(s) just before the bridge.

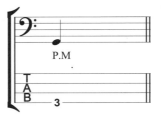

MUFFLED-STRINGS: A percussive sound is produced by laying the left hand across the string(s) without depressing it to the fretboard.

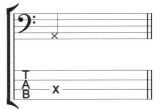

BEND (half step): Strike the note and bend up a semi-tone (half step).

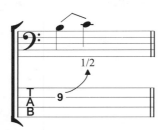

BEND & RELEASE: Strike the note and bend up as indicated, then release back to the original note.

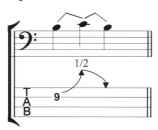

PRE-BEND: Bend the note as indicated then strike it.

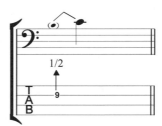

PRE-BEND & RELEASE: Bend the note as indicated. Strike it and release the note back to the original pitch.

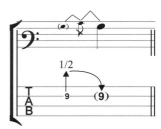

TRILLS: Very rapidly alternate between the notes indicated by continuously hammering on and pulling off.

VIBRATO: The string is vibrated by rapidly bending and releasing the note with the fretting hand.

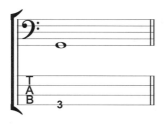

NATURAL HARMONIC: Strike the note while the fret-hand lightly touches the string directly over the fret indicated.

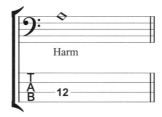

TREMOLO PICKING: The note is picked as rapidly and continuously as possible.

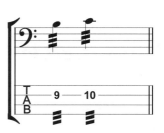

NOTE: The speed of any bend is indicated by the music notation and tempo.

Also Available

play BASS with...

Play Bass With...
LINKIN PARK
LIMP BIZKIT
SYSTEM OF A DOWN
P.O.D.
PAPA ROACH
MARILYN MANSON

Six Great Tracks...
ALIVE
BETWEEN ANGELS AND INSECTS
CHOP SUEY!
CRAWLING
THE FIGHT SONG
MY GENERATION
AM974974

Play Bass With...
BLINK 182
SUM 41
ALIEN ANT FARM
ANDREW W.K.
THE DANDY WARHOLS
AMERICAN HI-FI

Six Great Titles...
FAT LIP
FIRST DATE
FLAVOR OF THE WEAK
GET OFF
MOVIES
PARTY HARD
AM975634

Play Bass With...
BON JOVI

Six Great Rock Hits...
EVERYDAY
HEY GOD
IT'S MY LIFE
ONE WILD NIGHT
SOMETHING FOR THE PAIN
THIS AIN'T A LOVE SONG
AM976272

Great songs with <u>Soundalike CD</u> accompaniment tracks

CD Track Listing

1. *TUNING NOTES*

FULL INSTRUMENTAL PERFORMANCES
(WITH BASS)...

2. A.K.A. I-D-I-O-T
(Fitzsimmons) Universal Music Publishing Ltd

3. GET FREE
(Nicholls) Sony/ATV Music Publishing (UK) Ltd

4. GIRL ALL THE BAD GUYS WANT
(Reddick/Walker) Zomba Music Publishers Ltd

5. IN TOO DEEP
(Nori/Whibley) Chrysalis Music Ltd/EMI Music Publishing Ltd

6. THE MIDDLE
(Adkins/Linton/Burch/Lind) Cherry Lane Music Ltd

7. THE ROCK SHOW
(Hoppus/Delonge/Barker) EMI Music Publishing Ltd

8. NO ONE KNOWS
(Homme/Oliveri/Lanegan) Universal Music Publishing Ltd/Copyright Control

BACKING TRACKS ONLY
(WITHOUT BASS)...

9. A.K.A. I-D-I-O-T

10. GET FREE

11. GIRL ALL THE BAD GUYS WANT

12. IN TOO DEEP

13. THE MIDDLE

14. THE ROCK SHOW

15. NO ONE KNOWS

To remove your CD from the plastic sleeve, lift the small lip on the right to break the perforated flap.
Replace the disc after use for convenient storage.

5575 (24)
1 CD